MEANING OF MOUNTAINS

Mercury HeartLink

MEANING OF MOUNTAINS

poems

K. K. Cherry

Meaning of Mountains: poems
Copyright ©2011 K. K. Cherry

ISBN: 978-0-9827303-4-8
Publisher: Mercury HeartLink

Book design by Stewart S. Warren
Painting on front cover by K. K. Cherry

All rights reserved. Poems in this collection are the property of the author and may not be reproduced or transmitted in any form without permission from the author.

Mercury HeartLink
editor@heartlink.com

MEANING OF MOUNTAINS

MEANING OF MOUNTAINS

NATURE...

Snow...	*1*
Landslide...	*3*
India Ink...	*4*
Nightbirds...	*5*
Mountain Morning...	*8*
Wild Winds...	*9*
Milkweed Pods...	*12*
I Wear the Woods...	*13*
Fire...	*16*
Alpine Forget-Me-Nots...	*18*
Evening's Epiphany...	*19*
Snow Comes to the Mountains Tonight...	*20*
Silent Singing...	*22*

PERSONAL...

Daddy...	*27*
Exhibitionist...	*28*
Railroad Tracks...	*30*
Coal Room...	*31*
Moonflower...	*32*
A Sense of Closure...	*33*
My Husband...	*36*
Cape Cod Steeple...	*37*
About the Author	*41*

*Love forever to
Heather, Elizabeth, Tanner and Marley,
and to all those who have never lost touch
with their sense of awe and wonder*

NATURE...

SNOW...

I love snow
   the wild-wind-whipped snow
snow that blows with such fierce force
   atop mountain peaks
often throwing me off balance
   confronting me with vertigo
      a sense of not knowing
         which way to go...

I love the fast-falling snow
   snow that freezes and closes down
ice-covered electrical lines
   seizing... stopping...
bringing healthy halt... to a world going
   far too fast in the first place

I love the solemn... serene
   secret snow
snow that falls in six-sided
   vibrant ornaments
of white
   that light and lace
my long straight hair

I love the champagne powder snow
   blowing white whisper softness
as it drifts... delightfully... deliciously

    drawing me into a distant
dream-like state

I love the caressing snow
    seducing snow
bringing me into a sense
    of serene comfort
as I wander down empty streets
    devoid of any sound

And...
    I love internal snow
snow of solitude
    snow that brings echoes
        of past singing silence
as I listen to its quiet
    at the edge of a
        deep... darkened woods

This snow comes to me
    and blows through me...
        when I'm lost...
           and
              all
                  alone...

LANDSLIDE...

Inherent within the rambled rumble
   of rocks   echoed rhythms
reverberated their songs
   as they ferociously danced down
the mountainside

Scattered singings scrambled
    side... to side... to side

In awe   I stood below
   an obedient observer...
captivated   by their sheer power
    their screaming fierce force...
       their race down
   to the bottom

While then... suddenly... as though
    some unspoken command
       instructed them to
         STOP

There was silence
   complete
      total
         silence

INDIA INK...

    Jet black dark of India ink
spills across a vast expanse
    of evening sky tonight

    Devoid of any shape or form
until a small sliver...
    a sliced silver finger nail moon
appears between the saddle
    of a distant far off mountain

    I stand in muted awe
immersed in numerous nuances
    noticed never before

    When out of seemingly nowhere
comes a chaos of constellations
    creating a pneumonic
        symphony of India ink...

    A night time
      spill
        of sky

NIGHTBIRDS...

Deep within me
   I keep nightbirds

With winging
   singing
      silence

I fly
   I flutter
      I fling   myself towards
stirrings of steep
   ominous   darkened skies

Swiftly soaring
   with wings   I lift
      I swoop   I sing

Suspended in space
   for seemingly breathless
moments   I dance
   with the wind

Until soon... we two
   become one

Deep within me
    I keep nightbirds

In an embraced... darting motion
    we look down
upon slanted silhouettes... shadows that sing
    with a language
too difficult to comprehend
    from so far above

Then swiftly...   back and forth...
    upwards... towards a shimmering stutter
of stars   we glide

In and out
    we weave through hieroglyphics
of clouds...
    we sneak... we slither... we hide
we leave not a trace
    of our ride...

Though too soon
    a hushed
gossamer glimmer
    of light   begins to seep
gracefully across the landscape

I blink
    I glance off

      into space
          from this seemingly
drifting... dreamlike state

Yet knowing forever...

   Deep within me
     I keep...
        nightbirds

MOUNTAIN MORNING...

At the edge of
   the mountain stream
      frigid waters
         summersaulted...
        tumbled
         stumbled

Over whispers of hoarfrost
   covered branches
      shining with
         morning sunlight...
        they collided

With magnetic attraction
   they begged dance
      enticed to join
         with winter's landscape

This mesmerized
   mountain morning

WILD WINDS...

I stumbled while walking amidst
    seemingly "possessed..."
        wild winds that blew
their blinding... relentless rage
    with an insidious
        driving insistence

Their wind-whipped whirls
    muddled my mind
as they twisted and tossed
    and appeared imbued
with deliberate desire
    to blatantly blow me
off balance...

Wild winds within... wild winds without

Dancing... amidst swirled dust
    dizzied and ferocious findings
of fast-flying
    debris...
in vain attempt I tried
    to break free

Stunned and confused
    I stood... my mind
unclear... tired I clung fast
    to the secured base of a standing oak tree

My face flinched at the
    wild wind's rage... its fury... its forced
crazed and ferocious
    fling of rubble... brittle leaves...
hay and straw drilled straight
    into the side of a weathered
dilapidated falling down barn beside me

Far off into an often indistinguishable
    expanse of open landscape
I squinted... confused...
    while sand... grit... dirt....
singed my body... my bare
    exposed skin
outrageously the wind
    snarled... it snapped at
small branches... sticks...
    large limbs

Then through the sting of
    my scrunched and narrowed eyes
I blinked... I tried
    in vain attempt... to
decipher...
    to somehow identify

this swirled and whipped
   spiraled downward drawn
formation of particles
   of dust... that collided
      then decided in frizzled flare

These blurred and blinding
   siren sounding sensations
I experienced
   were in fact a Whirling Dirvish
my soul surrendered to

Wild winds within... wild winds without

MILKWEED PODS...

While I wandered through
    a distant mountain meadow
I came upon
    a muttering of Milkweed pods

They flung themselves
    wide open... songs
of white-winged
    poems... flew forth

I WEAR THE WOODS...

    Upon exiting a wide expanse
of morning meadow
    I enter the elusive... evasive...
yet familiar   welcome   of woods

    Behind glistening silver-beaded
threads of waterfall
    I bathe my thirsty body
then... drenched with freshness
    of morning

    Awakened... I step forth
stand upon a giant smooth boulder
    of granite

    Dried by a whisper of wind
a perfumed mist of damp rich earth
    falls all around...

    I float and flutter
surrounded by a flirtatious film
    of morning mist
that seduces and softens
    my supple skin

    I wear the woods...

    With brown eyes glazed
I roam around the woods
    I ponder... what shall I select
as appropriate attire for this day?

    Then I slither my body
into a dress of dusty lime-green lichen
    textured... with twigs   attached...
adding a sculptured   sort of quality

    Morning shafts of sunlight shine
upon a hushed soft lavender cluster
    of awakening Pasqueflowers

    A running ribbon of Reindeer Moss
ruffles the edges   of my cascading sleeves...
    then falls to a wild watercress
lettuced-edged hemline
    of my long-flowing   gossamer gown

    With bare feet   I attempt
to slither into the soft
    delicate beauty of two low-laying
Fairyslippers...   Calypso orchids
    endangered species   far too seldom seen

    Maiden's hair ferns
adorn my hair
    while the unfolded flurl   of a Rabbit's Foot fern
I eagerly select as enchanted earrings

I wear the woods…

   From the fast-flowing stream
I select a glimmering
   shimmer of stones

   Wet with rain-soaked seduction
I hold them in my hand
   they sparkle and shine
I attempt to decide

   Which luscious   dripping jewels
will be selected for   my necklace
   this delicious mountain morning

   Then… with threads of cobwebs
drawn from a dense stand of fir
   I weave them all together

   Satisfied with my appropriate attire
I saunter along
   the timbered trail of runway

   Deeper… deeper…
deeper into the darkness of forest
   I walk

I wear the woods…

FIRE...

Flames of fire flickered
   licked at stirrings
and laughed at February's
   frigid... icy... winter winds

While here
   amidst my mountain refuge
memories of far-flung
   dreams dwell

Memories I thought
   I had long since forgotten
embers eagerly flickered
   flared up
bringing light to thoughts
   believed I had
     held hidden... years and years ago

So... as with "through a glass darkly"
   I recalled... revisited... revised
vividly I remembered the pain...
   complete and with lucid clarity
     hurtfully aware again
that through this seemingly
   impenetrable darkness...

Recollected memories remained
    so deeply embedded…
impossible to explain… impossible to erase…
    from the deepest recesses
        of my
            conscious soul

ALPINE FORGET-ME-NOTS...

Far above timberline
   close to the top   of an undisclosed
      tumble of trail

I stumbled upon two merits
   of shining mica-encrusted stones

With unbounded enthusiasm   they embraced
   one tiny tufted cluster
      of mountain soil...
         holding fast to these lovely Lilliputians

"I remember you" I replied

A rare sprinkle   of Alpine forget-me-nots
   lifted their stare
of lavender blue faces   to mine

Yellow dappled stamens
   coupled inside a purity of white

We exchanged...   and admired glances
   amazed at the strength and stamina
within one another
     then I walked...
         on...

EVENING'S EPIPHANY...

Just before
   a rising
      gibbous moon

Exalted
   I stood
      observed

Slowly
   ascended
      luminous light... a flood light

Beyond the distant ridge
   outside my loft
      my mountain window

Mesmerized   I watched
   enthralled... knowing a scene

So stunning as this   is viewed often...
   though seldom "seen"

My worshipful eyes closed
   to this evening's epiphany

SNOW COMES TO THE MOUNTAINS TONIGHT...

She brings with her
   a silent duvet
      of feather-filled
         goose downed softness

Tenaciously she flies
   tirelessly   on and on
then tenderly
   touching... caressing twigs
she snuggles   into the crotch
   of forked boughs
nestles... nudges...
    beside fossilized boulders
      dated beyond
         thousands of years

As a gentle breeze blows
   she summons forth
      a dance

She drifts
    further...
       further...
          further...
             deep

Into a sound
   still... inner sleep
     hush...
        shh...
           shh...
               she sleeps

SILENT SINGING...

Snow falls
   in silent singing
elegantly embracing
     thirsty landscapes
       below

Softly...
   slowly...
      secretly...
         serenely

Composing her song
   with white
      muted insistence
       of memory

PERSONAL...

DADDY...

Four years old...
clad in blue and white striped
  OshKosh coveralls...
speckled red straw hat...

Barefoot... I'd run
down the dirt road...
  racing to try to beat my Daddy

Driving the tractor home
from working the fields
  all day long... corn... soybeans

A special whitewashed
painted fence post was
  our secret marked spot
"I'm gonna beat you Daddy!"
  I'd shout

Smiling... his big broad grin...
shaking his head... No...
  he looked as though
to challenge me...

But Daddy... Daddy always
let me win!

EXHIBITIONIST...

    When I was two
the thrashers came to our farm
    Illinois neighbors collected
together to help out Mom and Dad

    After a hard day working
the fields... lunch... of course...
    was the main meal

    Mama laid out quite the spread
baked beans in her favorite crock
    sliced ham...bread and sweet butter...
honey from our local beehive...
    all placed upon stretched
wooden tables... out back

    Always trying to contain
my wild-spirited ways
    Mama placed a
galvanized grey washtub
    beside the screened back door

    In my bright red bathing suit
I splished and splashed
    to the grinned enthusiasm
of the famished thrashers
    then... taking one step further...

I drew down my one piece...
   naked... I walked out of the washtub towards a horror stricken Mama
     "All wet Mama... All wet"

RAILROAD TRACKS...

    Remember when I used
to grab my bamboo fishing pole
    red bucket... bobbers...
a can of night crawlers
    headed down to Bloody Run
down beside the
    rapid ramble of railroad tracks

    With little money for food
I nested my newborn baby down
    into her Papa's faded red rain jacket
fished until I caught
    my limit of shimmering Rainbow trout

    Then... along creosote
railroad tracks
    that ran a few feet away...
I'd stick
    a-couple-a-pennies
to watch the engine smash them into
    smoothed out flattened copper

    I kept them for my baby...

    Remember?

COAL ROOM...

   In the bowels of the
basement
   of my Grandmother's house
was the coal room

   Fascinated by the
heavy black sooted heap...
   wide mouthed shovel...
sitting beside it... wrought iron holder
   mounted onto the wall...
"MATCHES"

   Amazed and in awe
I watched as the sooted coal
   was shoveled into the
open-mouthed...
   hot... burning furnace

   One small smoke covered
eyebrow window above...
   soot-covered... cracked...
never replaced

MOONFLOWER...

    The Moonflower   wound her way
around the fencepost
   from the ground...
she wound her way... up...
   passed curled weathered...
peels of paint
   wound until she found... the top
blued burst blurted forth...
   sang... this Sunday morn

    The man whose wrinkled...
weathered hands
   had sown her seeds
walked past   he stopped
   then... satisfied... he smiled
murmured... "Stay"

    His brown spotted hand tightened
around his wooden cane...
   glanced on down the road ahead
     and then slowly...
        slowly walked
          away

A SENSE OF CLOSURE...

Seized with strife and sorrow
    she wept her bitter tears
her saddened heart so heavy
    with memories embedded...
        etched... too deeply
            too much
                too have
                    to hold...

Her chasm... reopened
    exposed the sorrow
        like "salt to a wound"
            it stung

Drowning even deeper
    perplexed... she pondered
        punishment perhaps
            inflicted... but why?

Her sorrow seems eternal
    we listen to the sound
        of weeping
            tired tears...

Desiring... to bring this
    festering to the surface

         to silence
            the suffering...
She searched to somehow
    find a way
to stitch together
     tattered...
         torn...
             tired

Bit and pieces
   of seemingly forgotten
long lost memories

Rapid
    running
        remnants...
frayed pieces of fabric
     fluttered...

An internal wind
    stired
her soul
    with sensations
        that stung

Yearning...
    and with heavy heart
         she hungers to bring
             a sense of finality

to insistent... insidious
    scattered feelings

She craves...
    a cohesive...
        completed...

            Sense
                of
                    closure

MY HUSBAND...

When I was a child of four
my Mother opened our front farm door
   to an outside blazing bonfire

   She seized the worn out teddy bear
I treasured...
   with cotton clothes line wrapped
     around his neck

I used to drag him behind me
"He's my husband" I explained
   "Don't..." I pleaded "Please Mom...
     Don't... burn him"

   She snatched him from my grasp
tossed him to the leaping
   flames
while hot tears trickled down
   my cheeks

   I watched while he
turned... pathetically... into ashes
   I shuttered... unable
     to sleep that night

CAPE COD STEEPLE...

Wooden steps
   spiraled round
      upward
leading   to the top
   of the Cape Cod steepled church

Fourth generation   now
   family traveled   the Mayflower
Parker   climbed today
   faithfully he ascended
to pull the twined splintered
   gonged onged ong
of the clamor-clad
   casted iron bell
      this summer morn

He attended   it awaited
   he arrived
the Cape Cod steepled bell
   sits stilled
      throughout the week

Parker has passed on

ABOUT THE AUTHOR

Born "with mountains in the marrow of her bones," Colorado artist and poet K. K. Cherry believes strongly in the inherent language of landscape—a landscape there for all of us though listened to far too seldom.

While her work reflects an awareness, an appreciation and a reverence for nature... she states in her personal philosophy "I believe it is through the sharing of our creative efforts, we meet on the most common human ground."

See her paintings at www.KKCherry.com

www.ingramcontent.com/pod-product-compliance
Lightning Source LLC
Chambersburg PA
CBHW031244160426
43195CB00009BA/592